Words of Life Vol. II: Works of Christian Poetry

By Patrick Henry

All Scripture quotations, unless otherwise stated, are from the King James Version of The Bible.

Cover Design: Raw Designz Studios

3P: PH Pentecostal Publishing, LLC
New Albany, OH
3p-phpentecostalpublishing.weebly.com

In Memoriam

my dear friend,
Elder Kenneth D. Hutchinson, M.S.,
who taught me that my gifts,
including the gift of writing poetry,
ought to be used to bring glory to God.

In Memoriam

my sweet sister, Goose,
I see you in Angelique's face.
You're ever in my heart.

Contents

Foreword

Minister Patrick Henry, being a psychology major, is no stranger to the mental attributes of the mind, the spiritual mind specifically. He truly understands the conscious need for faith and dependence in an unshakeable and powerful entity that is too often dismissed in our century. It is not too often that academia and spirituality are combined to awaken a level of conscious spirituality that is too often ignored. Words of Life Volume II is just that, an artistic journey into the examination of the heart on its epic venture in life and in living.

The poetry within is both modern and timely. Although it is not written in sonnet form, there are instances of subtle rhymes and with a hint of the iambic pentameter while also written from a more modern "free verse" poetic mode, Patrick's poetry reflects the experience of a faith that is deeply ingrained, spiritually instructive, doctrinally charged, and informational to those who are believers of Christ and embracers of the Christian Faith.

At times the poetic verse appears to be written in the form of maxims or those philosophic constructs of Lao Tzu; the timeless principles of experiencing Christ in the written text is evident. At times the meter changes and there is a need to rhyme while at other times Henry merely shares his reflections on a faith that has obviously been a living faith and a support system in both life and living. The poetic style is a complex interweaving of verse and rhyme. At times it is a complex treatise of information that reveals the man-God Jesus and the mission He came to complete.

Henry is both an artistic poet and psalmist that shares the proverbs of life from an obvious perspective of one who has seen success and yet experienced those situations that cause others to be abated by the difficulties of life that are both uncertain and challenging. When reading the poetry of Patrick Henry, you will know both the man and the complicated journey of his life.

Bishop Derrick A. Reeves, Th.D., Ph.D., D.D.

Preface

Jesus At The Center Of It All

The theme of this second volume of Christian poetry can be stated concisely in one word that transcends and defies any fitting description by human language: JESUS.

The image on this book's cover effectively expounds upon this theme in a vivid and efficient manner. Each facet of the image conveys deep meaning and connects to why I write poetry. The black background represents evil/darkness of a fallen world that has been infected with the blight of sin after Adam's transgression. As the Bible teaches, death entered creation after Adam's sin in the Garden of Eden (Romans 5:14-21). Moreover, man was left with no permanent solution to the sin problem for ages, despite the temporary solution provided through the Law and its sacrificial system.

Into this void steps God incarnate: Jesus Christ. After living a sinless life before His Father and all mankind, Jesus went to Calvary and died in place of fallen mankind. His cross, shown on the book cover, speaks volumes. The horizontal bar of the cross represents humanity/human-human relations while the vertical bar represents God-human relations. Jesus, then, as He hung on the cross served as an explicit and vivid symbol of God reconciling mankind to Himself as He bridged the divide between mankind and God. Note also the ends of each bar of the cross. They are pointed, which symbolizes the end of a sword. Therefore, the horizontal bar also represents the sword that Jesus brings to family units. Faith in Jesus is the cause of conflict within families as few in each family submit to His plan of salvation while the rest of the family remain unsaved and antagonistic to God and His saints (see Matthew 10:34-35 & Matthew 7:13-14). The vertical bar then also represents the 2-edged sword of God's word which dictated that Jesus must die since the eternal Word of God had already declared that He would (Revelation 13:8). This vertical bar also represents the wrath of God against all sin poured out on Jesus at Calvary.

Let us now focus on the cover image's colors and their meaning. The white color of the cross symbolizes light, purity, and the holiness of God (John 1:4; Psalms 51:7; Isaiah 1:18; Revelation 7:14). The light emanating from the center of the cross represents pure sunlight, which in turn represents Jesus Christ (see Matthew 17:1-2), Who is the light of the world (John 8:12) and the brightness of God's glory (Hebrews 1:3). Furthermore, this Light is the light, the goodness, that pierced the darkness (which represents evil), while simultaneously containing no darkness (John 1:5; John 3:19-21). In other words, Jesus broke through the darkness without becoming tainted by darkness!

How does this image connect to the poems of this volume? I write because Jesus did not die and dispense gifts unto mankind (one of which being writing) for me to waste my gift writing about frivolous topics such as oranges and bicycles. Jesus did not die in my place for me to bury my gift in the sand and fail to use it at all. Jesus died and gave me this gift in order that I might use this precious gift to point the world back to Him (like John the Baptist: John 1:6-8). This book and the gifts used to create this book, would not be relevant without Jesus and His cross! I give thanks unto God! So, as much as I can, it is my duty and pleasure to utilize my gift for His glory.

How does this image connect to the title of this book? Quite simply, the focal point of this image and book is Jesus. Since Jesus is the Word Who was made flesh (see John 1:1-2, 14), any words of life are always connected to The Word of God: Jesus!

Incidentally, you will notice Bible verses at the beginning of certain poems. I do this to offer a way to introduce the poem. Thus, before reading a poem with such an introduction it might help to look up the Bible verse(s) mentioned prior to a particular poem in order to gain a deeper understanding of the poem. Similarly, you will notice Bible verses to the right of particular lines of some poems; these Bible verses are meant to provide a Scriptural basis for the main point of the particular line of poetry with which it is paired.

I hope you are edified by reading these words and all the poems that follow!

God Bless You & Yours,

Minister Patrick Henry, M.A., M.A., LPC

Prologue:

My Hope for Poetry

i write

words
wonderful words
wrought within

recollections
reminiscent of
winters & warm-seasons
once were, once-again

one writes words remarking upon
weeks-gone
weeks-now
weeks-next
ringing of revelations remarkable...
one-Lord oneness
one-Faith
one-Baptism
one-Love
one-Salvation won...derful

when Jesus relates words,

i write

Part I:

WHO IS JESUS?

JESUS Is…

Lamb of God (John 1:36)
Lion of the tribe of Judah (Revelation 5:5)
the Holy One and the Just (Acts 3:14)
Shepherd and Bishop of your souls (I Peter 2:25)
captain of their salvation (Hebrews 2:10)
great high priest (Hebrews 4:14)
door of the sheep (John 10:7)
the way, the truth, and the life (John 14:6)
Prince of life (Acts 3:15)
advocate with the Father (I John 2:1)
Wonderful (Isaiah 9:6)
Prince of Peace (Isaiah 9:6)
I AM THAT I AM (Exodus 3:14)
Immanuel (Isaiah 7:14)
faithful witness (Revelation 1:5)
good shepherd (John 10:11)
bread of life (John 6:35)
living water (John 4:10-14)
love (I John 4:8)
heir of all things (Hebrews 1:2)
the Almighty (Revelation 1:8)
Ancient of days (Daniel 7:9)
Holy One of Israel (II Kings 19:22)
Counselor (Isaiah 9:6)
light of the world (John 8:12)
resurrection and the life (John 11:25)
true vine (John 15:1)
man of sorrows (Isaiah 53:3)
everlasting Father (Isaiah 9:6)
author and finisher of our faith (Hebrews 12:2)

Branch (Isaiah 11:1)
root and offspring of David (Revelation 22:16;
Revelation 5:5)
The Word of God (Revelation 19:13)
Faithful and True (Revelation 19:11)
Sun of righteousness (Malachi 4:2)
mediator of a better covenant (Hebrews 8:6)
the Lord, which is, and which was, and which is to
come (Revelation 1:8)
Jehovah-jireh (Genesis 22:14)
Jehovah-nissi (Exodus 17:15)
Jehovah-shalom (Judges 6:23-24)
Jehovah-tsidkenu (Jeremiah 23:6)
Jehovah-rapha (Exodus 15:26)
Jehovah-shammah (Ezekiel 48:35)
Jehovah-raah (Psalm 23:1)
Alpha and Omega (Revelation 1:8)
the beginning and the end (Revelation 22:13)
the bright and morning star (Revelation 22:16)
Apostle and High Priest of our profession (Hebrews 3:1)
the only Potentate (I Timothy 6:15)
Son of man (Matthew 8:20)
King of kings and Lord of lords (Revelation 19:16)
Son of God...In other words, (Matthew 16:16)
Jesus is God. (Isaiah 9:6, I John 5:20; John 10:30)

Touch the Mystery
I Timothy 3:16

Hands small enough to fit on a cross
Yet large enough to carry all problems
soft enough to cradle my heart
skilled enough to orchestrate HIStory

A face that's common, calm, and comely
We made it undesirable
yet, wearing a smile belying wondrous warmth
a countenance brighter than the sun

Eyes, tearful from distance with the Father
Yet ablaze with zeal for Him
Viewing both the start and end at once
Peering into prideful hearts, and the depths of our
souls

Arms fragile enough to seize from pain and shock
as they stretched on a tree
yet wide enough to overshadow all willing
and strong enough to save

A heart that broke when Jews rejected it
While it pumped blood the same as ours,
Yet it is also unlike any other blood
For it bought our healing, protects us, cleanses us

All this and more
The mighty and the manly
The human and the heavenly

The earthly and the eternal
Woven together in a timeless tapestry

Perfection personified
Defying description and
Beyond understanding

Thus, we must receive Him
In order to…

Touch the Mystery

Victor. Blesser. Savior.

Victor.
As the Man of war
Over sin, death, satan - You've won
You've all power forevermore
And saints are Your sons

Blesser.
You've blessed us from the start
Because of where You stand
Given us access to Your heart
and not just Your hand

Savior.
Your cross is the Way
For fallen men to return to You
Risen the third day
So, we can reign, too

The Name
Acts 4:10-12; Philippians 2:9-11; Hebrews 1:3;
Colossians 1:15; Mark 16:20

Whose name heals sickness
Puts satan to flight
And alone can save souls

Whose name opens blinded eyes
Brings wholeness to maimed bodies
Restores leprous skin

Whose name belongs to the brightness of His glory
The exact expression of His essence
The image of the invisible God

Whose name turns muddy rivers into a
sin-cleansing flow
Trumps the power of death
Makes demons tremble in fear

Whose name is Immanuel, God with us
The fullness of the Godhead in flesh
When spoken ALL will bow, one day

Whose name is applied to the body of saints -
Who use it to work signs and wonders,
Confirming the truth of the true Word

The name of which i speak
is the name of the Lord
The name of God

That sweet name is…
JESUS!

Life
John 14:6; John 17:3; Proverbs 20:27

what is life?
is it security of money?
is it the allure of worldly power?
is it status and prestige with men?
is it lusts for the opposite sex?

Who is Life?
is He not security when vulnerable?
is He not the certainty of supernatural power?
is He not status and prestige with God?
is He not better than husband or wife?

while life for fallen mankind
likely consists solely of
money, power, prestige, and sex
Life for the saint revolves around
One:
JESUS Christ,
He is our Life.

for truly without Him
men are dead men breathing
existing, yet not alive
walking, yet going nowhere
ever learning,
but never coming to the knowledge of the Truth...

until He Who is Truth - Jesus -
saves us, takes up abode within us

Lighting our new candle
a metamorphosis
once a sinner, now a saint

now, with Him,
saints are living men breathing
existing, and alive
walking, and moving onward to glory
ever learning, and being led into ALL TRUTH

so
don't be content to merely exist
instead
receive eternal Life
in Jesus Christ!

Everything
John 1:1-4, 14-17; Colossians 1:13-17

You are I AM.
All things that were made
were made by You &
for You;
and I AM is *everything*

You are I AM.
All things that were made
were made by You &
for You;
and I AM is *everything to me.*

Nothing means anything
without Him Who is *everything...*
to me. If i had not the I AM,
Who is *everything*,
i would have nothing,
even if i had every-thing.

Why?
Because without the I AM,
Who is everything,
my soul would be bankrupt,
despite being filled with
money,
power,
sex,
education,
food,

and whatever else it would desire.

For even nothing is more than enough,
when paired with Him Who is everything

He is the I AM.
The I AM is Jesus.
& Jesus is God.
GET HIM…& you HAVE *EVERYTHING*.

Wisdom

1 Corinthians 1:20, 30

When the simple becomes profound
Intellect of the divine
Supernaturally juxtaposed with mine
Doubtless that it defies human logic
Obvious only after His revelation
Making man's version foolishness...

What is Wisdom?
Or rather, Who is wisdom?
JESUS CHRIST: the WISDOM of God.

The Revealed One
Hebrews 1:1-3; John 1:1-4, 14

First, He spoke to Adam
Then He made covenant with Abraham
He revealed promise of prophecy
To the fathers thereafter
And to the kings of the Hebrews
Usually by His prophets

But none of these insights
Excelled the prophecies
Concerning the Revealed One
The root and offspring of David
Likened to Moses
But superior to him
And to the angels
Forever our Great High Priest

For this One
Is the Revealed One:

After the flesh, son of Joseph,
After the Spirit, Son of God;

After the flesh, Rabbi of wisdom,
After the Spirit, The Wisdom of God;

After the flesh, a carpenter,
After the Spirit, The Maker of all things;

After the flesh, dead at 33,

After the Spirit, eternal;

After the flesh, a speaker of His Word,
After the Spirit, The Word of God.

Who is this One?
Jesus Christ -
the last revelation of God
To mankind
Now
saints merely
reveal the Revealed One
For there is nothing new
After His Son

Space/Time
Ephesians 4:8-10; John 1:1-3

Although He walked the earth
As a human
Yet He rides on the wings of the wind
And visits planets and stars
Across the cosmos

Although He came into the world
At zero
And departed earth in AD 33
Yet He lives in & beyond space/time
For He made the same

Although He may have He stood as tall
as a typical man of His day
Yet His height is immeasurable
And He fills all space/time...and beyond

Although He had flesh and blood
Experiencing His creation
with five carnal senses
Yet His Father is The Spirit
And His nature never had sin

Although we are born in sin
And shapen in iniquity
Yet He is The Way
For us to transcend the natural realm
And enjoy space-time...with Him

Although He is fully Man
Yet in Him resides eternity
And boundless space
Like a series of connected, furnished rooms
Each much bigger than the preceding one

He is Jesus Christ
The omnipresent God
Who can manifest Himself
Or remain a silent bystander
The Maker of space/time
And all encompassed therein

Good Father

Luke 11:2; John 10:30; Isaiah 9:6

Although mankind has been infected with sin
And many fail to accept the cure
Yet the Good Father…

Loves us, in spite of us, without condition
Provides for us, so we can never want
Intercedes for us, so the Accuser will not win

Forgives us repeatedly, when we feel unworthy
Extends grace, although we may frustrate it
Teaches us His ways, although we cling to our own

Sees us as those whose potential is fulfilled,
Though we currently fall short
For He knows what He can perform in us
Through His love for us that excels human
knowledge

Jesus is the Son
Jesus is the Spirit &
Jesus is this Good Father

Love.Light.Life.
1 John 4:8; John 8:12; John 14:6; John 17:2-3

Love
He is that warmth that fills my heart
at the thought of His face.
we're never apart;
He indwells my space.
so close i feel Him move
and hear His thoughts.
what a miracle the Lord has wrought!

Light
He is the spark
upon which true data rides.
this Light reveals truth
and truth never lies.
when His Light comes
all darkness must hide,
or run away.
indeed, it cannot stay.
for "darkness has no part in Me," (1 John 1:5)
is His testimony.

Life
He is Life eternal - in & beyond heaven -
for all who have no leaven
of false doctrine in their minds.
this Life leaves death behind.
for those who know Him
there's only life evermore.
since we've passed through the door (John 10:7)

we may fall asleep, but
we die no more. (John 5:24)

He is God.
God is Love.
God is Light.
God is Life.
God is Jesus!

Part II:

WHAT HAS JESUS DONE?

Cross/Words

Genesis 3:21; Romans 5:9-11; Revelations 13:8

Verse 1
Since the start of it all
His death was implied
The Lamb speaks truth to all
And defeats him who lies

Chorus
His cross speaks words
Do you hear what it says?
Having no mouth, yet its heard
By His blood that flows red

Verse 2
Because His cross brings together
sinner and Savior
Destined for fellowship forever
By our faith not our labor

Chorus
His cross speaks words
Do you hear what it says?
Having no mouth, yet its heard
By His blood that flows red

Verse 3
Cross/Words are kind:
"You're not left behind
With My love I will bind
Your heart, torn in pieces

Freeing you, your malice ceases."

Bridge
His cross speaks healing
His cross speaks hope
Its blessings have no ceiling
Its miracles have no rope...
Or strings attached
Needing a transfusion
His blood is a match
Let there be no confusion
There is no catch

All who're willing, come
There's room for you
Breathe new life in your lungs
Sinner, Jesus loves you too

Chorus
His cross speaks words
Do you hear what it says?
Having no mouth, yet its heard
By His blood that flows red

Bridge
All who're willing, come
There's room for you
Breathe new life in your lungs
Sinner, Jesus loves you too!

The Gospel: The Power of God Unto Salvation
Romans 1:16

Join me on a ride
Back to ancient times
We talking bout the past
Some say antiquity
When you ended the year with a "B" and a "C"
The latter representing the last name of Him Who
came
And took the blame
Restored the lame
Undid man's fate past the father of Cain (Romans
5:12,14-15)
The only Man ever with sin-free blood
In His veins

i'm your tour guide
Sit back as i tell the story
Of how this God/man Jesus died
And rose unto glory

Back then capital punishment was worse than death
You might gasp in your breath
When you learn how life left
Or desired to run away
From its earth container
When these heinous acts were inflicted
On these, the convicted

i digress
Of the Lord's death, hear the remainder

A life begun in a manger
And begun to "end" as they bore nails in
His hands
Both of His feet
Of the pain Jesus felt
i cannot speak

He was sinless to the day
They strung Him up on the tree
High on Calvary
The blood flowed down His extremities
(it shoulda been you and me)
instead Jesus took the rap for man's sin
and did so willingly

the cost of sin is death (Romans 6:23)
yall hold on peep
the price He paid, He paid for all
His Love's just that deep

So as Christ hung like a criminal
Darkness covered the land (Matthew 27:45-50)
The Father had placed the sins of man
Upon His only Son, the true sacrificial Lamb

But indeed, this Son was @ His peak
So, the other sun the Father had to hide
Know you not that if the Son of Man be lifted up
He'll draw all men to himself (John 12:32-35)

This precious life He did give up
And relinquished it to man

Then Jesus ROSE FROM THE GRAVE
And LIVES today
To complete the plan

Of redemption for man
Who, through Christ, can
overcome the sin
That dwells within
the flesh you now see and feel
hell fire won't consume it
please believe, its real

…that your sin brings to u death (Romans 6:23)
so, while u have breath
choose life
the Way of this Christ
obey the 38th verse of Acts 2
THEN
let His Spirit work holiness in you

that when this life is done
and the next one begun
you'll have overcome
sin and death; a world plagued by satan

you'll have what he lost through rebellion:
LIFE
with God Almighty in heaven

In Jesus' name, Amen.

Come, Just Come
2 Corinthians 12:9-10; Matthew 11:28-30; John
4:10-14; Acts 2:38

"Need fully-filling food?
Come.
Need thirst-quenching water?
Come.
For no more unforgiving fathers…
Come, just come.

Need strength-releasing weakness?
Come.
Desire Light in darkness?
Come.
For no more unhealed wounds…
Come, just come.

Need sin-stopping power?
Come.
Want a soul-satisfying Savior?
Come.
For no more fabricated, false doctrine…
Come, just come.

Come to the Living Waters
Which move while you're still
The Waters of one baptism:
Natural waters to cleanse sins-past,
Super-natural waters to prevent sins- future.
Come.
Come,

Just come.
AND FIND REST FOR YOUR SOUL
Gain My Life
As you give Me yours...
Only when you come."

Love,
Jesus

Sweet Communion
Isaiah 40:31; Ephesians 5:30; John 15:7; 2 Peter
1:3-4

Come
Commune with Me
Tell Me all about
Your concerns
Your dreams
Confide in Me

Let Me impart
My Life into you
From My Holy Spirit
Then to your spirit
Then to your soul
A beautiful exchange:
Your cares for My nature

Use My name
My angels of Light
My blood
Speak
Life-giving, demon-chasing words
To reconstruct your world -
Both within and without

Love on Me
In sweet intimacy
Tell Me
the sentiments of your heart for Me
For I AM your God

And you are Mine
I AM in you
& you are in Me
So
Stay
Here
With Me

Give Me access
To all that is you
At all times
And I will do the same -
What glory you'll find

As we enjoy
sweet communion
forever.

Like Kind
Romans 5:12-21

By man sin entered
By Man sin was conquered

By man sin and death were *born* in us
By Man they were defeated

By man dominion was lost
By Man dominion was regained

By man authority was abdicated
By Man all power was awarded

By man we entered the curse
By Man we can enjoy the blessings

By man blood was spilled
By Man sinless blood was applied

By man we lost the battle
By Man we *can* win the war

By man we died
By Man we *can* LIVE

man is Adam and his children
And Man is the Son of Man:
Jesus Christ
By Whom all that was lost
Or defiled

can be redeemed…
Including mankind

All because One Man died
To undo the horror
Of the error of another man
Man-for-man: like kind

Paid in Full
2 Corinthians 5:19-21; Colossians 2:13-15;
Hebrews 9:28

you had a debt you could not pay.
He paid a debt He did not owe, so that
you can have a reward that you could not earn.
Thank you, JESUS!

After... a While
1 Peter 5:10

Your heart's been broken
BUT
After...a while

A messenger of satan has attacked you
But
After...a while

Loneliness lurks near you
BUT
After...a while

Your debt dwarfs your income
BUT
After...a while

Friends fall away
And
Your kids are being turned against you
And
Shame knocks at your door
And
Deliverance seems like a faint dream
BUT
After...a while

GOD will
Mend and *complete* you
Without surgery

Stabilize you
Without your 5-year-plan
Strengthen you
Without bodily exercise;
Found a new you
Through rebirth and renewal

So, wait on Jesus
Patiently in faith
And watch
your promised prosperity
Meet you in your present
After...a while

The *Fixer*
Colossians 1:20-23

Jesus can fix it.
Do you believe?
Jesus can fix it.
Just receive.

Jesus will fix it.
Yes, He will.
Jesus will fix it.
Just be still.

Jesus fixed it.
Yes, He has.
Jesus fixed it.
It came to pass!

YOU

i love YOU,
worship YOU,
confide in YOU,
pray to YOU.
bow before YOU -
even when it hurts -
submit my will to YOU.
cherish YOU.
i'm not my own,
i belong to YOU
praise YOU,
magnify YOU.
No longer my own god
i exalt YOU.
commune with YOU.
Nothing else matters
without YOU,
so, my everything is YOU.
cry to YOU.
wait on YOU,
indebted to YOU.
My heart beats for YOU.
Though YOU're a Spirit
i'm never alone with YOU.
press toward YOU.
No one else died for me
so i give my life to YOU.
listen to YOU,
i'm in covenant with YOU

i'm only something
Because i'm in YOU
Thus, there's no me
Without YOU, Jesus

Dark Fire
Matthew 8:12; Luke 16:23-24; John 3:18-19

Oh, peculiar paradox
Furious flames
But no light
Oppressive heat,
But no warmth -
As sensed by the heart
Not the body

Such is eternity
For those
who don't believe
God,

Who's a consuming fire
Which both burns the impure
In us.
And gives light
To direct our way
Through a dark world
As it did for Israel.

i digress
Of the dark fire
i will speak.
It burns
But doesn't consume
Your body.
Rather it *consumes* your mind
with: tormenting terrors;

Mistakes made;
Iniquities inflicted;
Sins submitted,
And entered
Into your record.
Forever
You'll toil in sorrow.
Unless
Repentance is your response
To your sin.
In this life
Choose Christ
That you might not succumb
To the second death
And be enveloped
In dark fire.

For Jesus
has made
The Way
Through His cross
To escape
the peril of perdition.
And instead
Reside in the Light
Of the Son
In heaven
Amen.

Part III:

WHO AM i IN JESUS?

Foes...then Friends
Ephesians 2:1-3; Romans 5:1; Psalm 34:8

When i was Your foe, You weren't far from me still
On the cross, for my sins You were killed
In my ignorance i warred against You
Your grace looked at the old me, but saw the new

Every err, every mistake, every sin
Your blood covered all and brought me in
Whom the devil called lost, You called found
Though i was Your foe, in iniquity bound

i was wrapped in death, You brought life
i was an offense to You, now no more strife
Between You and I, once a foe now friend
If I hold to faith till the end

In, with, & through Jesus I now have peace
As Your friend not foe, ALL blessings are released
And via faith and love they're accessed
Meditating always on His Word yields success

Retire from *team foes* and be His friend with me
It's better than this life...come taste and see!

me, *in relation* to YOU

YOU are the Father; (Isaiah 9:6)
i am Your son.(1 John 3:1)
YOU are the Jasper; (Revelation 21:10-11, 19; 2
Corinthians 4:7)
i am Your earth. (2 Corinthians 4:7)
YOU are the King; (Revelation 19:11-16)
i am Your appointed.
YOU are the Potter; (Jeremiah 18:6)
i am Your clay.
YOU are the Bishop; (1 Peter 2:25)
i am Your disciple.

YOU are the Drummer;
i am Your drums.
YOU are the Marksman;
i am Your arrow.
YOU are the Warrior; (Exodus 15:3)
i am Your weapon.
YOU are the Physician; (Mark 2:17)
i am Your medicine.
YOU are the Word; (John 1:1, 14)
i am Your preacher. (Luke 4:18)

Thank YOU, Jesus!

Be Content
1 Timothy 6:6; Philippians 4:11

Will you be humbled,
Without being disgruntled?

Where there's power-producing pain,
will you endure,
While keeping soul and body pure?

Although tears are your *friends*
To the heartache there's seems no end.
And the stress threatens to rend
Your mind
And vex your soul.
If only your issues
could be buried in a hole...

Alas they can't.
And respite feels scant.

Although life's problems won't relent,
Follow His command & be content.
And towards godliness be bent,
Much you'll gain after much prayer spent.

Only through Jesus
Who's dispensed His grace.
His will may not always please us
But when all else fails
Knowing even your human life is frail.
With Jesus, you'll still smile

And suffer another mile
Along Pain Street.
So, let godliness and contentment meet.

Because Christ is your Life
Since He's always Good
You can ever be content, no strife.
And bear Good Fruit
From His Spirit within.

Thus, be content with His face & heart.
You'll win in your end, as surely as at your start!

Cactus
John 4:10-14

What is a cactus?
Is it not a…
Fortress of fortitude
A paradoxical and pleasing pillar of a plant
Thriving mostly in deserts
Fully sustained by meager water supply
That would kill most of its distant brethren
Armored to ward off enemies
Yet arrayed with beautiful blooms

Who is a cactus?
Is *he* not a…
Faith-filled fortress of fortitude,
A Pentecostal paradoxical pillar
Like a plant who thrives in deserts
Fully sustained by rivers of Living Water,
Who gives Life to all his willing brethren
An Apostolic, armored to ward off the Enemy
Yet arrayed with beautiful blooms of God's
blessedness

Who is the cactus, you ask?
i am…
as long as i trust in the
I AM. (John 8:58)

Where i Belong

Where the pitter-patter of little feed abides
Where my wife rests by my side

Where the devil is RIP
Where discord loses to unity

Where godly potentials are fulfilled
Where, in His presence, we are still

Where our roles are forged through pain
Where the Lord sends the latter rain

Where finances from the Father flow
Where my mind shows his growth

Where dreams are resurrected
Where souls are perfected

Where prophetic visions are given
Where, to this end, we are driven

Where Love guides   (I John 4:8; John 16:13)
Where upon the flesh we won't rely

Where my heart sings a new song
Where i ... *belong.*
HOME.

POWER

Power to heal
Power to bind
Power to yield
Power to cast mountains into water with words
Power to create action with verbs
Power to dispel spirits unclean
Power to commune with the Holiest Being
Unseen

Power to lay hands
Power to stand
Withstand
Stand with
Power to share my brother's burden - "It's my shift"

Power to raise the dead
Proclaim death dead
Power to overcome sin
Power to prove the truth of the Word
Said of Him
By Him
It's Him
Power to deem atheism absurd

Power to live
Power (to self) to die
Power from on high
Power the same
as when the Spirit first came
in tongue-flames

and they preached His name
Power of JESUS...

Let it reign
It must reign
It shall reign
Praise His Name

POWER
Part 2

Power within
Power over sin
Power without
To conquer satan's doubt

Power of His Spirit
Linked to mine
Brand new; i tap in, & feel it
Both sublime & divine

Power so great
He transcends description
Through Him
i defeat all opposition
Please believe, it's not fiction

Power of living Fire
That lights my new candle
Bringing satan ire -
The Spirit he can't handle
Or resist
Once i partake
Satan must cease and desist

Power of God
It's real
And can dwell in you
Please repent, dear friend
That's what you must do!

Radio Heart
Psalm 37:4; Ezekiel 36:26; Colossians 3:2; John
8:58

Set the frequency of your Radio.
Hear the Music.
Dance to the beat.
Repeat.

What is the radio?
Is it not your heart?
Which, before the divine Transplant
Struggled to attune to AM -
The frequency of the I AM.
The function was present
But the music was typically faint, muffled, and hard
to discern
So instead you *chose* the worldly FM dial
And mindlessly danced to its hypnotic, sensual beat

What is the radio?
Is it not your heart?
Which, after the divine Transplant,
NOW has the capacity for crystal clear AM
reception
So that you can clearly hear the Music of the I AM
And lock eyes with the Savior
In the loving embrace of the best slow
dance...EVER

BUT
You must choose

You must daily tune in to AM
To hear the music of the I AM.

As you set your Radio to AM daily,
Reception of the I AM's Music becomes
Clear
And loud in its meaning -
Resounding, thunderous -
yet quiet in its volume
Filling your ears with heavenly melodies
That quench the deepest longings of your soul
So, you return daily for more
And more
And more
until
You no longer desire the FM frequency.
Instead you daily...

Set the frequency of your AM Radio.
Hear HIS Music.
Dance to HIS beat.
Repeat.
ENJOY!

Winter & Spring
Ecclesiastes 3:1

It's winter now
With the harshness of the snow
The danger of sharp, slippery ice
The perils of angry winds

But
Know ye not
That the white snow reflects the brilliance of His
Son
When winter lingers,
glaciers – majestic and mighty – cut through rocks,
like your heart
Eroding its wickedness, making it tender, fit for
Word-seeds
These glaciers move mountains of your world
Rocks of Gibraltar that stood for ages

For hope is like water vapor
Unseen
Until the frigid winter season
Transforms it into water, then ice and snow,
Into faith, visible by what it produces.
The same faith that brings with it God's grace, and
God's righteousness

Know ye not that Jesus is the God of seasons…even
the winter
For it prepares the way for spring to spring
forth…in your life

Once your spring season manifests,
Remember the God Who kept and molded you
through the winter
A winter that made you fit to receive His spring
season

Lest you say in your heart, like the Children of
Israel:
"I believe I caused the spring
That I fashioned the sun to rise
That I impregnated the clouds with live-giving
water
Which, when delivered, yields the motions of new
life in the earth –
New marriages, with the same spouse
New wealth, when the supply exhausted
New grace, when it seemed you were unable
New health, when infirmities plagued your body
New faith, when doubt crept in unawares.
That I clothed the lilies and roses in a glorious array
of shades
Which offer a sweet-smelling savor."
If so, your pride will pollute your world
and yield longer, more vexing winters to come...

Instead, praise and worship Jesus -
The God of seasons
By remembering your winters
During your springs
And your springs
During your winters

Worship While You...

Worship while you *war*
Worship while you *wrestle*
Worship while you **rest**

Worship while you *hurt*
Worship while you're *harmed*
Worship while you **hear**
God

Worship while you *cringe*
Worship while you *cower*
Worship while you **call**
Jesus

Worship while you *weep*
Worship while you *wait*
Worship while you **WIN**

Worship while you LIVE... forever!

A Poet's Poem For Caterpillars

A Poet's Poem...
i looked at black poetry
& what did i see
tales about you
some about me
allegedly
But little about He

For within the stanzas, lines, and rhymes i've read
Of certain poets, alive and dead –
Phillis, Paul L., Langston, Gwen, and Sonia –
Who paint characters so familiar, they might
knowya
Coloreds
Negroes
Niggers
Blacks now
Our creativity, intelligence, strength, and know-
how we endured, persevered
While lassoed and chained yesterday
Yet today it's the same
With a diffr'nt name
As freedom bells ring-rang
4th day 7th month
a holiday they claim

i buff my glasses again
Take a 2nd view
But that's all i see
Of the goodness within you and me

Told by these poets
And that's only when i squint long enough to
behold it
After i sift through the
Pimpsplayersdrugscussingdepression
And celebrated debauchery
Portrayed as our reality

Maybe for you?
If so
i pray
You have an ear
to hear
And eyes
to see
My reality
A new life, just the King and me (John 3:5; II
Corinthians 2:17)

For (Caterpillars)
i write words that give life to the life i live
Abundant that is
As one of His kids
Much different from the one's they see –
Fellow black poets of history –
In contextuality

My reality – changed
The life i live ain't the same
Neither am i...why?

Well i believed on the name

Of the Man who was slain
(not by establishment, to appease whites' disdain of
brownskins who came - 'untamed', in chains, to die
insane and in vain)
NO…

i believed on the real Lamb (John 1:29)
whose plan was to take a stand
then the fall
pay the price for us all (Romans 6:23)
His grace + our faith
To answer the call
& follow the Way of the Light
so tall
for you see the life you live is not yours at all:

you cuss
you lie
have sex w/out her hand
you may drink, or smoke
medication is your plan

for deep down you know
the person of whom the poets write
the black man/woman –
strongdynamicamindsobright –
as the mirror gazes @ you
it shows a life void of life
suffocated by the cares of this world
and succumbing when the world ends…
or just your time on it

i digress
of my life was i speaking
how i became a new being
it was the Lord's provision
for all whose decision
is submission
to His Plan (Acts 2:38)
to save man
with His right hand
as He did me
& given of His Spirit and Mind (Acts 2:4; Joel
2:28-29)
another life changed –
slave made free
i was once the caterpillar
slimy, crawling on its belly
many moving feet; a frenzy
yet traveling not
Bound
to the constraints of this world –
greed, lust, other evils thereof –
NOW,
a butterfly
Sailing above the struggle for justice and meaning
that plagued those leading men & women
Looking instead to the Son-King
Whose warmth abides within
And to His treasures above…

His name? "Jesus!" they say.
He's written a poem of your life too.

Won't you read what He has to say? (show crowd a Bible)

The Tipping Point
Acts 1:8; II Peter 1:1-4

And i received power
After i received Him
No more will i cower
Nor should i sin

By intuition of my new spirit
i confirmed the wisdom of God
By His grace i did hear it
And satan was robbed

Of a prized pseudo-pawn
For of my true strength i now know
The deceptive lie is now gone
And forever i will grow

As i grasp the weight
Of the divine nature within
A greater power He did not create
For there's none greater than Him

Who commands realms seen and not
From particles in atoms
To the space/time plot
To realities i can only fathom

Who rose Himself from the grave
Who is the author of all mysteries
i can't die, if i stay saved
In Him, my ignorance is history

This power is *now within* me.
Thank God I now understand.
This shift of thought is the tipping point,
And part of God's plan.

The Shepherd's Sheep
Psalm 23:1-6

You're my Shepherd
Lead me on
As i submit to You

Through my old mind
i am prone to stray
But through Your nature
i happily follow
Your every
(in)direct direction

You open the gate
i pass in and out
Finding all i need
To grow:
my mind
my heart
my will
my body

Although You may feel distant at times
Yet i can hear Your voice:
Your thoughts that interrupt mine.
Because i trust You
i follow
Though wolves lurk,
Snakes lie in wait,
And inclement weather threatens
(all screaming fear) ...

Still my steps are ordered,
You direct my path

For Jesus You are
My Good Shepherd
You hide me from harm
Unless it's for my good
So even my pain
Effects my progression
In You
To You
For You
Until…
One day
i bask in Your presence
Forevermore
Amen.

About the Author

Patrick Henry, M.A., M.A., LPC is a Chicago native and two-time graduate of Northwestern University, where he earned a bachelor's degree in Psychology and a master's degree in Counseling Psychology. Most recently, he earned another master's in Developmental Psychology from Loyola University Chicago. Patrick has written poetry for close to 20 years, and he has written solely Christian pieces since shortly after Jesus saved him in 2002. From 2002-2017, he attended Christ Temple Apostolic Faith Church in Chicago, Illinois where he served as a teacher in Sunday School and in D.R. Bell Bible College and as a drummer. Patrick now attends Endtime Apostolic Christian Holiness Church under the pastorate of Bishop Derrick A. Reeves, Th.D, Ph.D., D.D.

In addition to writing Christian poetry and books, Patrick is a trained counselor, teacher, and preacher. He is founder/CEO/chief editor at 3**P**: **P**H **P**entecostal **P**ublishing, LLC. He can be reached at 614-522-9624 or at pathen238@gmail.com.

Acknowledgements

I want to thank everyone/everything that made this book possible – family, friends, mentors, and my tests/trials. To not neglect anyone, I will avoid listing names. You all were used to help create experiences in my life that God used as "material" for this book. And finally, thank You Jesus for giving me this gift of writing and allowing me to share it with the world! I love you all with the love of Jesus Christ!

The Non-Created Christ

John 1:3; Colossians 1:16-17; Hebrews 1:3; I
Timothy 3:16

ALL things were made,
Are made,
Will be made,
Except the One
ALL things,
Except the Christ…
Space,
Time,
Heavens,
Gravity,
Angels,
Orbits,
Sun, moon, and stars
Indeed, the universe,
ALL were created
By and for Christ

Yet He is non-created
For the One has always been
And always will be
Therefore, He is I AM
For as Creator
He transcends all created things
Even reality itself

This Christ

Holds all creation together
in Himself &
by His rhema Word

Although He was born of Mary
Yet, birth merely manifested Him
For He alone is eternal:
the I AM

The One is He
He is God &
God is Jesus of Nazareth:
The non-created Christ